Re:CONSIDERING

THE COST
OF COMPASSION

Tim Costello

I0163035

a. Acorn
Press

Published by Acorn Press, an imprint of Bible Society Australia, in partnership with the Centre for Public Christianity.
ACN 127 775 973
GPO Box 4161
Sydney NSW 2001
Australia

www.publicchristianity.org

ISBN 978-0-647-53093-1 (pbk)
ISBN 978-0-647-53094-8 (ebk)

Editor: Kristin Argall
Cover and text design: John Healy

About the Centre for Public Christianity

What is the good life?
What does it mean to be human?
Where can I find meaning?
Who can I trust?

In sceptical and polarised times, the Centre for Public Christianity (CPX) seeks to engage the public with a clear, balanced, and surprising picture of the Christian faith. A not-for-profit media company, since 2007 CPX has been joining the dots between contemporary culture and the enduring story of Jesus in the articles, podcasts, books, documentaries, and other resources we produce.

We believe Christianity still has something vital to say about life's biggest questions. Find out more about our team and the work we do at www.publicchristianity.org or follow us on Facebook, Twitter, and Instagram.

CPX CENTRE FOR PUBLIC CHRISTIANITY

About the author

Tim Costello AO is a well known social justice advocate. He is a Baptist minister, former CEO of World Vision Australia, and currently a Senior Fellow for CPX and Executive Director of Micah Australia.

CONTENTS

INTRODUCTION:
IT'S COMPLICATED

Who is in favour of compassion? Okay, I see a lot of hands. Presumably all the bleeding hearts and soft heads.

Let's test that with another question. Who is *against* compassion? Gosh. That number wouldn't even fill a telephone box.

Where are the hard-headed true believers in the market? The staunch defenders of merit and hard work? Okay, there you are – but you're still unequivocally for compassion. Oh yes, I remember US President George W. Bush's 'compassionate conservatism'. I shouldn't reduce this to political affiliation.

So whether right or left, religious or secular, Confucian or Christian, carnivore or vegetarian … it seems we have a consensus: compassion is good.

Well if we all agree on this universal ethic, how hard can it be to overcome our divisions and build a better world? After all, we're all on the same page here, right?

Not so fast

As a young church minister in St Kilda, I was used to the knock on the door from desperate people. This was well and truly before St Kilda was discovered by the professional inner-city elite; that happened over the next decade. In the mid-1980s, it was a catchment area for runaway kids, drug-addicted teenagers, street working women and their pimps, and de-institutionalised mentally ill and homeless adults.

As a fresh-faced minister, I saw my whole enterprise as motivated by compassion. To me, our small Baptist church was essentially a compassion centre, and the congregation we were building was in the business of helping people.

Declaring compassion our core business was like flashing a neon sign: OPEN. The street traffic to my door proved the advertising was effective.

I heard a lot of tragic stories, and gladly helped a lot of people. But I also learned there were people who could travel Australia on their stories, gifted actors at spinning a yarn. One of my early encounters was with a man who stood weeping at my door. He was down from Queensland, he told me, where he'd fled a nightmare. He had

2

been driving his car, towing a boat, and it had jack-knifed and rolled in heavy fog, killing his wife. He had buried her but, seeing her framed picture on the mantelpiece of his home, grief had overwhelmed him. He could not face his loneliness, or the painful memory of the accident. He'd left, and now his money had run out and he was homeless. He knew he could get work, though, if he just had somewhere secure to stay for a bit.

I was drawn in with genuine compassion. Seeing an ordinary-looking Aussie bloke in tears with obvious love for his deceased wife moved me deeply. I got my wife to scrounge him a sandwich to eat, and he left with whatever cash I had on hand to get a hotel room for a few nights, courtesy of our church. (This was before the days of credit cards, when I could call and book him a room.)

About a week later, I was sitting in a meeting with other local ministers, and one of them began sharing about an encounter he'd had that week – same man, same story, same generous result. Another person chimed in to say, 'Yeah he tried that on me, so I checked out a few details. They didn't all add up and I got suspicious. The bloke got angry, swore at me, and obviously left our church for yours. I should have warned you!'

Part of me was furious. I realised I'd been duped. My legal training made me feel especially incensed

– I of all people should not have been taken in! I wanted never to be deceived again, and resolved to limit my credulity, kindness, and compassion.

The outcome was that my compassion all but dried up. I found myself becoming suspicious of everyone, and that same legal training made me want to cross-examine every story to the nth degree. I knew it meant that some people genuinely in need were missing out on help they desperately needed from me.

Slowly, I arrived at a compromise. I would remain alert to a scam, but also be compassionate, and accept that sometimes that meant I would get ripped off.

In the end, it was only money – compassion was a scarcer resource.

A compassionate life?

Looking back, I realise that the people I admired most, even as a kid, were the people who could be described as kind or compassionate. I aspired to be that kind of person.

My father, for example, could be a strict disciplinarian at home, and I often feared him. Yet there was another, surprising side to him. I knew he cared deeply about people. As a teacher, I remember him putting himself out for a widow, teaching her son in his own time. I saw the same quality in other men in our church, who would give up their Saturday to fix the gutters or fence for a neighbour who had suffered unemployment or separation. (The word my parents would darkly mutter was 'desertion'.) No fuss, no lofty words, just practical hands-on compassion. Financial generosity was unremarkable, disposed of with a 'don't you worry love, we'll fix up this bill.'

Sporting heroes aside, my childhood heroes were those who took risks to care for others. Often they were missionary doctors, nurses, and teachers who went to serve people in India or Africa and toil with the poor. They would come home on furlough and show their slides at our church, telling stories of helping people excluded from their communities because of leprosy or blindness or other disabilities. I heard stories of girls forced into early marriage and how education gave them a way out. I was riveted and inspired. Indeed, in my later teen years, when my school peers were aspiring to be businessmen or merchant bankers, deep down I wanted to be a missionary – not that I'd noise that abroad at school.

I was drawn to ordinary Australians whose lives radiated compassion. They were on my radar. Something in their understated yet burning passion to serve the vulnerable struck me as the highest calling. I now recognise that their compassion left an indelible imprint on my life.

But I also understood intuitively that the whole business was complex. Within the religious circle that shaped me, compassion was the spiritual pinnacle, the highest prize – but it was not just natural and automatically there. It required formation and focus. Sunday sermons on the Good Samaritan or on Jesus' words in the Gospel of Matthew set a high bar: 'Lord, when did we see you hungry and feed you, naked and clothe you, or in prison and visit you? When you did it to the least of these my brothers and sisters, you did it unto me.'

Looking beyond my own community, I could see that compassion was widely admired but also contested. Our experience of it is tricky. Who has not felt some inner conflict when walking past someone on our streets homeless and begging? Unless we have stifled all compassion, most of us wonder at times: do I make eye contact to acknowledge their humanity? But if I do, and I get drawn in, I'm faced with new dilemmas. Having seen a human face who has seen me, can I just walk on by? If I throw a few dollars, will it help or will it just feed an addiction? (And who carries cash these days anyway?) Should I stop and offer to buy them a coffee, or share a conversation that embraces our common humanity? After all, this is a fellow citizen, who as such has some claim on me.

These feelings are rarely resolved, and whatever decision we make there is no neat solution. To pretend I have not seen them is to deny my own truth. To engage may be to get more involved than either time or finances permit. Compassion is tricky!

And for me, this ambivalence has gone far beyond the local. I built a career on the hope that our universal esteem for the idea of compassion could translate into social and global renewal. But even when as CEO of World Vision Australia I was surfing the wave of the 'compassion industry', travelling to disaster zones in poor nations, I knew I would see both magnificent compassion pouring in and malicious malevolence pouring out. Foreigners were moved by the plight of strangers and wanted to help them, yet locals could be untouched by their neighbours' pain and give in to corruption and self-interest.

I knew, too, the risk that the humanitarian cavalry riding in to fix things could often trample on dignity and local practices. We responded from compassion – but not pure compassion. We were also responding to our own needs and drives. Our need to be seen as compassionate; our need to be needed; our assumption that our systems of help were right and superior. An assertive 'take charge' mindset could displace being a humble presence. Relational compassion could easily be subsumed by professional competence.

Darkly, I often reflected that responding to a natural disaster is like an oil strike in our industry. The agile get there immediately and plant their brand flag, do some media to show that we're responding, mail out to supporters for help and start raising dollars. A disaster was the value proposition that attracted donations and kept the wheels turning. Compassion literally is the oil that greases the aid sector's wheels.

In short, compassion as a universal resource has remained an enigma. If compassion is so treasured, why is there still such conflict, inequality, and suffering in our world?

Why do the self-sufficient and well-off show such anaemic compassion levels? Why the compassion fatigue?

How deep do the roots of our compassion really go? How can we become more compassionate? And do we really want to?

It's a lot of unresolved questions. Compassion turns out to be far from simple. This book comes out of my own ambivalence, and also my hope.

1. IS IT NATURAL?

For most of us, the reaction *but what if that were me?* feels instinctive. If it were me in that situation, how would I like to be treated?

Empathy for others – even for those unlike us – is a distinctive human trait, though many believe it's shared by other animals. In circumstances where a 'survival of the fittest' principle might otherwise rule, our capacity for imagination, for putting ourselves in another person's shoes, has the power to override more fearful and reactionary instincts.

And yet the human imagination also facilitates cruelty. Fear of the other, demonisation, scapegoating, torture – only the human animal seems to take pleasure in inflicting pain. As the writer Marilynne Robinson has put it:

The fact, or at least the degree, of human exceptionalism is often disputed. In some quarters it is considered modest and seemly for us to take our place among the animals, conceptually speaking – to acknowledge finally the bonds of kinship evolution implies. Yet, in view of our history with regard to the animals, not to mention our history with one another, it seems fair to wonder if the beasts, given a voice in the matter, would not feel a bit insulted by our intrusion. History is the great unfinished portrait of old Adam. In the very fact of having a history we are unique. And when we look at it we are astonished. Only in myth or nightmare could another such creature be found. What a thing is man.

Unless you are a sociopath, all of us experience feelings of sympathy and identification, and we give them the name compassion. It is reflexively human to be moved by the plight of another and feel the urge to do something about it. We see this as spontaneous, emotional, and natural. But how tenuous are these responses? How easily crowded out by other 'natural' human impulses – by fear or selfishness?

Laughing at ourselves

A *Seinfeld* episode nails our own shallowness, virtue-signalling, and ulterior motives when it comes to compassion.

Jerry, George, and Elaine have the realisation that one day they too will be old and, as unquestionably good and compassionate people, decide to volunteer to visit the elderly. Their intentions start out honourable, but the purity of their motives becomes increasingly dubious.

George ends up arguing with his cheery old man on his very first visit. The 85-year-old is not afraid to die and never thinks of death, while George is totally obsessed with his own death and assumes everyone else is also. Since he doesn't get the conversation or perspective he was hoping for, George abandons his resolution. When the others express their shock that he has given up so quickly, George explains that he comes from a family of quitters and that quitting is the one thing he is very good at.

Jerry doesn't fare much better. He only endures the irascible old man he's visiting in order to get his hands on the priceless Al Jolson records he says he's throwing out. His 'compassion', it transpires, is undergirded by self-interest.

Elaine is bringing companionship to an elderly shut-in but finds herself nauseated by the woman's large goitre. She tells the others that it's like a second head. Although we never see the woman's face – only the back of her head – we hear her frail voice and see Elaine's face, her shock and disgust. We can all identify with her incoherent attempts to pretend she's not repulsed, and her acute embarrassment when asked, 'Is it my goitre that puts you off?' 'No,' Elaine stammers, 'I wish I had one too.'

Elaine is all of us, unable to manage her feelings, her compassion evaporating in fumbled civilities, awkward and ridiculous. She just wants to get out of there and tick this off, duty done – that is, until the woman matter-of-factly drops into the conversation that she was once beautiful and, as a younger woman, Mahatma Gandhi's lover. The framed picture of the two of them that she hands to Elaine confirms it might just be true. Suddenly, Elaine sits down and engages differently, the goitre forgotten. A real person with a fascinating past has emerged. Elaine's new-found compassion emerges from entering someone else's world, seeing them as 'just like us' – having a story worth telling, worthy of love and respect – but also from the spice of the story and the cachet of being able to repeat it.

Still, Elaine reminds us that there are very few people you cannot love once you hear their story. A show about nothing has a lot to teach us about our hidden selves. As we laugh, we are also confronted with the inadequacy of our own fund of compassion for others.

The great reversal

Thankfully, our culture rarely questions the right of victims or the poor to a claim on their fellow humans, especially on the powerful. It rarely questions the legitimacy of social justice movements. If anything, we sometimes now find ourselves in a race for victim status in order to present our claims.

You can blame Christianity for making all this plausible.

A little historical digging reveals that while human sympathy may be natural, the claims of compassion are far from automatic. To protest in ancient times that you were poor or a victim would be to admit weakness and invite contempt. The brilliant 19th-century neo-pagan philosopher Friedrich Nietzsche understood this well, dismissing Christianity as a slave morality and advocating a return to classical values. He saw compassion as 'a weapon in the hands of the weak'. It had inverted the normal order of things by exalting the poor:

Christianity has taken the side of everything weak, base, ill constituted. Christianity is called the religion of pity. One loses force when one pities [has compassion]. Pity on the whole thwarts evolution which is the law of selection. It defends lives disinherited and condemned. In every noble morality it counts as weakness. Aristotle, as is well known, saw in pity [compassion] a morbid and dangerous condition which one did well to get at from time to time with a purgative. Nothing in our unhealthy modernity is unhealthier than Christian pity.

That would receive a cheer in the Graeco-Roman world, which lionised the strong and powerful, and thought that those who suffered probably deserved it within the logic of the rational universe.

How did we get from there to here?

The shock to the Western world's system was delivered by Jesus, who proclaimed a reign of God where the weak and meek flourish, and whose non-violent challenge to the hierarchical rule of imperial power seems to have been what got him killed by the state. The story that took hold of the Roman Empire over the next few centuries was of a defenceless, suffering god who became human – not as a king, but as a peasant rabbi who said 'Blessed are the poor' and humbled himself even to death on a cross.

The cross was used by the Romans as a demonstration of power and contempt over their wilful subjects. It not only enforced order but publicly humiliated those who questioned their legitimacy. Even public or videotaped beheadings by ISIS are quick. But crucifixion was agonisingly slow and dragged out over two days for the sake of spectacle. There was no greater shame imaginable in the ancient world; it was the final statement of who is superior and who is in charge.

The death of Jesus, then, was a subversion of military and political might. Understood as a deliberate act of self-sacrifice – no mere historical accident or miscarriage of justice – ultimately it morphed the cross from an instrument of power over the weak to a symbol of the power of weakness. The shock is that God is on the side of the victims and those most humiliated. It is a great reversal.

Compassion had new content. Contested content, certainly – but whether atheist, religious, or somewhere in between, this is the story that has framed our approach to the vulnerable ever since.

Re:CONSIDERING

2. IS IT PRACTICAL?

In the majestic and (to modern ears) sometimes bizarre idiom of the King James translation of the Bible, the language of compassion is *gut* language:

> But whoso hath this world's good, and seeth his brother have need, and shutteth up his *bowels of compassion* from him, how dwelleth the love of God in him? (1 John 3:17)

There is something natural, something even visceral, about how the suffering of other people affects us. But compassion is incomplete without action, and if we don't choose to suppress it or water it down, it will stretch and change us – often not in ways we anticipated, or wanted.

I read the poignant story of a New York doctor who was working at a Brooklyn hospital in March 2020 as the coronavirus started to ravage the community there. He wrote about working with a 100-year-old Hasidic lady who had the virus. He knew she would die, and was desperate to send her home, but her blood pressure dropped so low they had to keep her in hospital. Her son kept phoning the doctor who, overwhelmed, finally had to tell him frankly, look, she's 100 years old with pneumonia in both lungs. She's not good. She's not going to do well. He wanted to speak with her, but the doctor was too busy.

Ten minutes later, the son called again and was told his mother was now unconscious. He asked the doctor for a favour: he knew he couldn't be there with her, but it was very important he say a prayer for her – could he hold his phone close to her so he could do that?

The doctor knew he had ten other very pressing things to do in that moment. But, out of respect for the 100-year-old woman, he stopped what he was doing, put his phone on speaker close to the woman's ear, and told her son to speak. The son started to pray the Shema, the Jewish declaration of God's unity. In that moment, the doctor noticed the numbers tattooed on the old woman's arm. As the son cried and prayed, time slowed down for the doctor. It woke some forgotten emotion in him, and he felt restored to himself. Afterwards, the son thanked and blessed the doctor, who thanked him in turn. It had been a transformative moment.

Doctors in a pandemic are required to be transactional. In places with the worst spikes of COVID-19 infection, reports emerged of having to choose patients for life and death, triaging who would receive an ICU bed and a ventilator and therefore who would miss out. Unavoidable but devastating decisions to preference the young and let the elderly die.

In such a transactional climate, a phone call from the son of a 100-year-old patient could only seem like an interruption, a distraction from younger, saveable lives on the ward. Yet his instinct for compassion led him to take the call and allow himself to be stretched beyond the comfort zone of his medical expertise. The compassion he showed made for an experience as significant for him as for those he helped.

Keeping social distance

On Anzac Day 2020 I visited my 90-year-old mother, in lockdown in her nursing home. With no contact allowed, I sat outside and we talked on the phone, looking at each other through a glass door. She was wearing my late father's World War II medals, and she told me she had read the poem 'In Flanders Fields' over the PA system to all the residents. Her father – my grandfather – had been wounded on the Western Front, and she had memorised that poem as a child. Later I tweeted a photo of us, with palms matching on either side of the glass, to mark the occasion.

It was an image that resonated for many. The cruellest part of the pandemic was the separation from loved ones who are frail, especially at the moment of death – heartbreaking stories of people dying alone, without the touch of others. I lived with the fear that I might not see and physically touch my mother again. There is an existential guilt to this: no one is born alone, and no one should ever die alone – especially the one who gave me life.

Separation anxiety is universal, part of our human condition. The Genesis story of Adam and Eve being expelled from the garden for their sin, whatever its full meaning, certainly means separation. Separation from one who sustains, protects, and loves us will inevitably leave us feeling abandoned. Such anxiety – the fear of being abandoned, adrift in a world without meaning, subject to fate and death – accompanies us through life. We sublimate it by pursuing hyperactivity in work and various addictions, or even provoking conflict to assert our superiority and mask our vulnerability. We have our ways of anaesthetising the pain of existential separation.

Compassion accepts that we are not truly separate from others. So much of what passes for compassion in our world remains transactional: I help you, I hope that will make me feel better about myself, but I am not up for too much challenge. I keep you at a polite or professional distance. But as that New York doctor discovered, compassion asks more of us than we bargained for, and also gives us more than we bargained for. It confronts our shallowness and breaks through our attempts at 'social distance'. It is the eye of pity and solidarity with chronic human anxiety.

Suffering with

The literal meaning of the word compassion is *to suffer with*. If many of the impulses that we call compassion are cheap, emotional flares that die away quickly and leave nothing and no one changed, the real thing demands more. It means caring enough for someone to share in their suffering – to join them in it. It is costly.

The early Christians, believing in a God who in Jesus cared enough to join us in our suffering, showed indiscriminate care to others. Their gospel proclaimed, in the words of the Apostle Paul, that there was 'neither Jew nor Gentile, neither slave nor free, nor is there male and female, for you are all one in Christ Jesus' (Galatians 3:28). The divisions that we humans use to mark us off from one another were made nought, and everyone bestowed worth by virtue of being made 'in the image of God'.

During the third-century Plague of Cyprian, with thousands of people dying every day, it was reported that Christians opted not to flee the cities but rather stayed to nurse the sick. Many died as a result. (Many others embraced this new religion, seeing their compassion and their fearlessness in the face of death.) Their care was costly. Founding hospitals that were open to all, this community began to transform how we think about the sick and afflicted.

The coronavirus pandemic made us realise how vulnerable we are as humans, and how foolish we are to erect distinctions of superiority. Those who put their lives on the line – who bravely chose to *suffer with* the afflicted – were often the poorly paid nurses and other healthcare workers who showed indiscriminate care and throbbing compassion. We saw plainly who and what we really value, who and what counts as 'essential'.

I always quietly try and see someone else as made in the image of God, but in COVID-19 lockdown I found myself suspiciously eyeing others in the supermarket, seeing not an image-bearer but a potential threat to my health. To maintain physical distance was an act of prudence and (yes) compassion for others. But I was reminded of the need to continue to open my heart and refuse to see others as separate from me.

It is not convenient. But there are existential wounds that only compassion can heal.

Compassion fatigue

The first time I was confronted by what I call utter human evil was in Darfur in 2004, in the desert areas of Sudan. World Vision flew me in and, driving through the bleakest landscape imaginable, I saw a horizon of tents emerge. Barely a tree remained in sight. The earth was flat, the sun bore down mercilessly. There were clumps of blown bush debris but little else.

I was taken to the registration area and introduced to the people in charge. Then I was able to talk via translator with several of the women (it was nearly all women and children). Their husbands and fathers had either been killed or had disappeared in the night to try to escape being rounded up. Many of the women had been raped and injured. I spoke with some who had lost children to malnutrition on the long walk to the camp. All the work of an Arab militia armed by Khartoum and known as the Janjaweed. It was human evil writ large.

I was only there for about four days. So many asked me to help them, to save their children. I felt utterly helpless. I knew that soon I would be escorted back onto a plane, and back in the comfort of my own home within a day or two. I could escape. I felt gutted by guilt at leaving people who saw me as their one forlorn hope.

By the time I got back to Melbourne, I had also contracted a bowel illness, so when the media contacted me I was not in a good state. Still, the burden of what I had seen, heard, and smelled weighed too heavily. I dutifully went off to front the waiting media. Somehow, a question cracked my professional veneer, and I felt tears down my cheek. It was all too much. Usually I could talk and cover my emotions – I can talk anywhere – but now I couldn't keep it all from overflowing. There I was, on national television, sobbing, unable to control my tears as I spoke of the horror unfolding in Darfur.

My illness lifted, but the emotion associated with that experience remained. I carried those memories with me, and at various times in the years since I have been unexpectedly overtaken by the same emotion – even on happy occasions, when what I am saying and doing is not at all congruent with my tears. It is as though there is a reservoir of guilt and impotence that remains within me from those days, and the walls I have built up around it spring a leak. It takes very little to trigger the stories I heard then, to make me wonder how those women are now and whether their children are alive.

Is this compassion fatigue or burnout? I don't think it is. Compassion fatigue has been called the negative cost of caring, and is common for those who work on the front lines of healthcare, child protection, or emergency response over a protracted period, as well as for those being a friend or carer to someone with a chronic illness. Symptoms that the emotional resources to continue engaging with such suffering have run dry include an inability to function in one's usual way, insomnia, anger flare-ups, and loss of concentration. This is a serious issue, and I know how important it is to build in respite for carers so that their reserves can be replenished.

What I experienced after Darfur, though, does not map onto this. I did not tire of going to places of need. I could absorb fresh traumas, organise assistance, do the work necessary to encourage others to respond. I still felt able to function in the face of the distress I witnessed. I think it was not compassion burnout but compassion 'burn in'. What I was seeing and hearing took me to a deeper level. Encounters like this both deepened the wells of compassion and moderated my expectations about what could be done to truly help.

I have found that the trick in life is managing expectations. Too high and you burn out, disillusioned; too low and you do not try hard enough. In Darfur, I learned the difference between what I think of as the hardware and the software of helping. For those women, there was no safe place. There was no village or home safe from the pillaging of the Janjaweed; forced out, there was no reliable water or food supply; there were few police and those were poorly paid and generally corrupt; and so here they were, stuck in a refugee camp in a desert. All of these wrongs needed fixing, but I could do so little.

But I could do something. People want solutions, but even more, they want to know that they are seen and heard. If technical relief programs are the hardware of compassion, the software is relationship – giving people dignity in the opportunity to tell their story. Having the patience to be there, to listen and to recognise that deep humanity and hope is birthed only in relationship. My faith tells me that simple presence is as important as aid solutions. I must look into someone's eyes and say: God knows your name and so do I. I know your story and I will tell others. You are not alone, whatever the intractability of this terrible situation.

I carry the grief and the lingering guilt from these encounters and many others. Compassion is costly. It cannot leave us where we were before.

3. IS IT NECESSARY?

Ridiculous as it sounds, I once appeared alongside the Dalai Lama as a guest judge on *Masterchef*.

We had to do the filming before midday as Buddhist monks, who rise early, fast after the midday meal. I was invited to begin by saying a blessing on our food. The filming then proceeded but hosts Matt, George, and Gary were having some difficult moments. Every dish brought out for us to taste and adjudicate on met with the same response from His Holiness. He would pronounce it very good, followed by his trademark giggle. When asked what he liked, he would say he liked the bread accompanying the dish! Pushed by one of the hosts as to whether he preferred this dish to the last contestant's offering, he would say, 'No, no, just the same. They are equally good.'

The logic of the show demanded comparisons to heighten the tension and make for a contest. Observing the panicked looks of the increasingly baffled and exasperated hosts, I said, 'Your Holiness, as a Buddhist you are not allowed to judge, are you?' I saw astonishment flit across the faces of the others as he replied, 'No, we must never judge. When it comes to food, we monks go from house to house with our food bowls and are deeply thankful for whatever someone gives us.'

Judgment, like competition, is a compassion killer. Seeing their program format evaporating before their eyes and wanting to help out, I said, tongue in cheek, 'Unlike His Holiness I am a Christian and we are into judgment. So I liked this plate and think it is better than this one.' I wish I had not said this just to salvage their show. Maybe a moment of false compassion?

The pursuit of happiness

We in the secular West have told ourselves a particular cultural story. The uncontradicted goal of most humans is to be happy, and surveys indicate that we believe happiness comes, firstly, from being loved, and following that, from being healthy and wealthy. We know relationships are important, but we also think of autonomy and self-sufficiency as core to a fulfilling life. Dependence and vulnerability will lead to unhappiness; being self-invented, productive, and competitive in the market will secure a base level of happiness. Once we've shored up that base, compassion and generosity are a kind of optional extra, the icing on the cake.

I call this the health/wealth-to-happiness story. It is so invisible and plausible in our thinking as to go almost unquestioned. We pass it on to our young as a cultural meme, urging them to follow this path. Yet I can introduce you to a lot of wealthy and healthy people who are seriously unhappy.

On that ill-fated *Masterchef* episode, one of the female contestants had served up dumplings that were undercooked, with raw flour embedded in them. Honestly, they were horrible. And she knew she had failed. Crying, she blurted out, 'I am so in awe of you and wanted to cook something simple and elegant to express my deep respect for your simplicity.' Then her tears overwhelmed her – perfect for television. The Dalai Lama looked at her kindly and said, 'Come closer and give me your hands.' He held them and calmly looked her in the face and said, 'You know what? It really does not matter. It doesn't matter.'

Compassion poured out of him. Both she and I suddenly forgot the cameras and what was, after all, a shallow reality show in this moment of raw reality. Fancy that! A moment of true compassion in an artificial TV studio. Of course it did not matter, except in a world trivialised by ratings and the superficial construct of a contest. I do not know what happened to that contestant, but I could see joy flood her face in that moment. 'Look for a way to lift someone up', says Elizabeth Lesser, a popular figure within the wellness movement. 'And if that's all you do, that's enough.' His Holiness did it seamlessly.

Here was an exiled leader whose Tibetan people have suffered terribly. He is one of the most vulnerable leaders in the world, and he models dependence and compassion. Here was somebody without any of the trappings of our dominant story who was nonetheless happy. And the reason? He had learned the secret of compassion – a compassion that transcended the surreal limitations of the *Masterchef* arena, and the drama of constant competition.

'If you want others to be happy,' the Dalai Lama has said, 'practice compassion.' And the quotation continues: 'If *you* want to be happy, practice compassion.' If he is right, then compassion is not an add-on, the by-product of a happiness secured by achievement. That is backwards: it is instead happiness that is the by-product of compassion.

Competitive compassion

If our personal pursuit of happiness goes off course when we treat compassion as merely an optional extra, the same is true in the political arena. Compassion is not a luxury for when the economy is booming and we have something to spare for those who aren't doing so well. It is foundational to how we organise society, the glue that holds together strong and weak, old and young, and offers opportunities to flourish to all. Do we live in a web of mutual dependence and connection, or in a race to secure what limited resources there are for me and mine?

Because compassion is so universally esteemed – at least superficially – it is also near-universally deployed to frame some of the most contested issues on our political agenda. Where do we stand on issues of treatment of refugees, foreign aid levels, euthanasia, unemployment and disability support, indigenous rights, climate policy and animal rights?

Sometimes it becomes a compassion competition. People who are passionate about animal rights can darkly mutter that it might be good if Gaia had her way and more poor people died out, meaning more species would be protected from population growth. Those of us who are big on human rights can have a blind spot for animal rights. Pro-life and pro-choice advocates both claim compassion, but with different priorities – for the wellbeing of the foetus or the autonomy of the mother. Euthanasia is the same. Some are deeply concerned for the suffering of those with a terminal illness, and others fear a cultural shift where doctors sanction death in some cases rather than unequivocally preserving life, and the vulnerable may feel pressure not to be a burden. In many ways, political responses that we label right or left reflect innate wiring, where our compassion responds to different priorities and comes from different perspectives.

In our manoeuvres to out-compassion each other, compassion for one another is almost inevitably lost in the process. We find it difficult to credit those arguing against us with motives of compassion at all. We solidify into tribes, and begin to see other people as the problem. If greed and the desire for self-sufficiency is a block to compassion, so is self-righteousness.

And the fault lines are confusing. I am conservative when it comes to being pro-life and suspicious of euthanasia, but when I apply the same perspective to capital punishment and criticise harsh law-and-order responses, I am seen as left. I am called left when I advocate welcome for refugees, recognition that Australia Day has a shadow story of dispossession, and measures to limit coal and carbon even at the cost of jobs and economic exports. But I am apparently a right-wing moralist when I rail against why Australia has, to our shame, 20 per cent of the world's pokies and the highest gambling losses per capita of any country, by a long way. But I do recognise that those who disagree with me on all these issues are not lacking in compassion; they are prioritising other aspects of wellbeing, concerned with jobs and with personal choices.

Compassion is a necessity, not an add-on, for our lives as individuals and our life together. If we cannot practice it in the way that we engage in the political process, then our efforts to shape society itself to be more compassionate will be less and less effective.

4. IS IT POSSIBLE?

Most of us will look at someone we consider very compassionate, like the Dalai Lama, and assume that they must have been born that way. We practise our professional skills or our art or music to become better exponents. But though we agree we should all be compassionate, practice seems a foreign notion here. We exercise our bodies to be healthy and our minds with educational courses. But I know of few courses teaching compassion. Maybe we assume it should just be natural – either you have it or you don't. Training seems contrived and artificial.

But is the Dalai Lama just a person born with a huge dose of compassion? I think he is hardly likely to agree with that. His lifelong formation has focussed on cultivating a more mindful and compassionate outlook.

So if most humans have compassion, however deep or shallow, is it a capacity that deepens with practice? How do you become a more compassionate person?

What you believe matters

The main route humans have taken to deepen their compassion is religion. I know, I know. I won't shirk the failures of religion and religious people – when they have been judgmental and ranged themselves on the side of the -isms like racism, sexism, and species-ism. But given that most of the world today is deeply religious, and that the secular West has only been what we might call secular for some 200 years, religion has been the main laboratory for cultivating compassion in human life.

All of the world's major religions have something to say about compassion. Buddhists, for example, are taught that they must practice compassion towards all sentient beings. In many Buddhist countries, all young men have a short period as monks. While other societies prize university learning and some, like the Israelis and Swiss, have a couple of years of compulsory military service, this universal religious formation program highlights a different priority in values. It is literally their compassion-deepening course.

Hinduism, too, advocates compassion for all life forms as part of one large universal family.

In the Hindu hierarchy of gods, Brahma, Vishnu, and Shiva are compassionate – but the most compassionate is Vishnu, the sustainer of the universe. In Islam, Allah's names include Rahman, 'compassionate', and Rahim, 'the merciful'. A Muslim therefore begins every prayer in the name of Allah who is Compassionate and Merciful. Jews and Christians, too, proclaim a God who is compassionate and gracious by nature.

If you believe in an intelligence or spirit behind the universe, what you think they are like will matter for your practice of compassion. In Graeco-Roman religion, the gods had little interest in right or wrong, or in humans at all. They were powerful enough to mess with the world, but largely uninterested in it, and had to be appeased and their hostility kept at bay through sacrifice (sometimes human sacrifice). In such a world, showing compassion to others may or may not be right or prudent, given the time or circumstances. But to define God in terms of compassion and justice was to assert that these things were part of the fabric of the world he had made, and that to act in this way was therefore always both rational and right.

There have always been competing visions of what reality is like and therefore whether or not compassion is a logical response to it. In the third century, the influential philosopher Plotinus, the founder of Neoplatonism, wrote that those who suffered deserved their suffering:

> an expressed principle does not look in each case to the present, but to previous periods and to the future as well, so as to assess their worth from these and make slaves of those who were previously masters ... and to make poor those who misused their wealth ... and if they previously killed people unjustly, to be killed in turn ... It is certainly not by chance that a person becomes a slave nor does one just happen to become a prisoner or be abused physically for no reason, but a person who was once the perpetrator of what he now finds himself suffering ... From what we see in the universe, we must conclude that the everlasting order of everything is something of the kind.

If you live in an 'everlasting order' like this, compassion is surely thrown away.

In 2006 I was in Mumbai, at the Taj Mahal Hotel (which two years later would become the focus of an attack by an extremist Islamist group in which at least 167 people were killed), giving a press conference with Adam Gilchrist, who was a World Vision Ambassador and was in Mumbai with the Australian Test cricket team. He had visited his sponsored child that day in a Mumbai slum.

I have never seen such an enormous press pack. Cricket seriously matters in India. But the main purpose was for Adam to explain why, for him, there are even bigger things in life than cricket, and to talk about India's poor. He turned to me at one point to ask how many Indian children in poverty were sponsored by Australians. I said more than 4,000. He then asked World Vision India's National Director how many Indian children were sponsored by Indians. Awkwardly, he said it was less than 1,000. Adam was incredulous, saying to the press, 'I know how much wealth there is in this nation, and I see the poverty everywhere. This is surely not good enough.' Australians can be blunt! He added that he was going to speak to Sachin Tendulkar (an Indian cricket god) about why this was so.

He was right to ask the question. Part of the answer lies in the caste system which, while illegal under the Indian constitution, is religiously embedded in people's thinking. Karma, which is the law of cause and effect, looks at those from a lower caste who work in dirty jobs or as domestic servants and sees the explanation for their present suffering in the wrong choices they made in a past life. While a neat answer to the religious and philosophical challenge of suffering, the karmic picture of social fatedness is a serious block to compassion. It allows the Hindu rich to literally not see the beggar at the door of their mansion.

We all have a picture in our heads of what

the world is like and how it works, even if it's an unconscious one. And this picture will tend to have either a nurturing effect or a withering one on our instincts of compassion toward others.

Albert Einstein, the Nobel Prize-winning physicist, once wrote in a letter to a grieving father:

> A human being is part of a whole, called by us the 'Universe', a part limited in time and space. He experiences himself, his thoughts and feelings, as something separated from the rest – a kind of optical delusion of his consciousness. This delusion is a kind of prison for us, restricting us to our personal desires and to affection for a few persons nearest us. Our task must be to free ourselves from this prison by widening our circles of compassion to embrace all living creatures and the whole of nature in its beauty.

For Einstein, my sense of myself as separate from other people and objects is a 'delusion' – *actually*, if we could only realise it, everything and everyone is connected, and learning to feel and act in line with *that* reality is a moral imperative. Commitment to a picture like this one, whether it comes from a religious or a secular perspective, is necessarily a matter of faith. It cannot be proven.

This is clear too in one of the most influential modes of ethical thinking of our own time: utilitarianism. Not all utilitarian thinkers are atheists, and not all atheists are utilitarians. If, through the eyes of the atheist, the material universe is all there is and evolved human life is a kind of 'accident', then right and wrong are essentially human constructions. One option then could be to look at the natural world and see survival of the fittest and the dominance of the strong over the weak as the way things do and therefore should play out. But utilitarianism holds that, if we as humans experience pleasure as good and suffering as bad, the most ethical choice is the one that will produce the best outcomes for the greatest number of people.

The atheist and utilitarian philosopher Peter Singer is a leading exponent of the effective altruism movement, which is particularly concerned with applying rational measurement to the challenges of global poverty. It asks the question: How can we, individually and collectively, do the *most* good? Singer's book *The Life You Can Save: Acting Now to End World Poverty* sets a simple test: if you saw a child drowning in a pool, would you not plunge in – even if it meant ruining your nice clothes, for example – to save a life? If you would not hesitate to save the child in front of your eyes, why do we not see the life of the child living overseas in poverty and dying of preventable causes the same way? We can easily give out of our abundance to save the lives of others. Why would an ethical response extend only to those who are proximate and not to those who are distant?

Singer has certainly been one to live out his talk, giving away 30 per cent of his income each year to charities like Oxfam. His reasoning banks on that spontaneous instinct we all have to help the person suffering right before our eyes, and then appeals to logic to extrapolate out to include more and more people in the circle of our compassion. Yet he accepts that his ethical notions of the good cannot arise from naturalism of 'what is'. A universe that lacks a compassionate God to impose order, meaning, and moral duty, has no purpose. 'What is' cannot lead to an ethical 'ought' and to values like compassion.

Singer believes that the good exists beyond science and naturalism – that there are objective values that exist outside of subjective feelings, just as mathematics is objective and exists apart from human emotion. Humans have evolved a consciousness and rationality that can choose ethical purposes for themselves, and human agency which opts not to reduce suffering when we have it within our power to do so is a moral failure. Whether for the effective altruist, the Neoplatonist, the Buddhist or Hindu, or for me as a Christian, the level of our moral commitment to compassion will flow from our understanding of what the world is really like.

Theory vs practice

But we all know that people sometimes, perhaps often, don't act in line with what they believe (or say they believe). If we are honest and self-aware, we will know that our own actions are not always consistent with the values we claim.

I can certainly own this on behalf of Christians. Let me mention two examples of where Christianity has momentously failed its own creed – and what it has looked like when that creed does translate into action.

Although Bishop Gregory of Nyssa was railing against slavery in the fourth century, it took until William Wilberforce in 1789 to begin the campaign to outlaw it. Christianity, like most of the world, could not imagine how to act on its principle of 'neither slave nor free'. Economies were built on slavery. How could you prosper without it? It was only when slavery became racialised with the African trade that it slowly became clear, first to small pockets of the church like the Quakers, that this system also violated the radical racial inclusion ('neither Jew nor Greek') of the early church. The bill for abolition that Wilberforce introduced at Westminster must have sounded as crazy to the English as an Australian MP saying, 'Today I introduce a bill to abolish all fossil fuels'. It was an act of moral vision which chose compassion even under threat of economic suicide.

A second example is gender. Along with neither Jew nor Greek, neither slave nor free, Paul's first-century prescription of neither male nor female remains a struggle in many parts of the Christian church. Men rule the church. I remember being in the Solomon Islands watching the seven bishops of the Anglican Church do gender violence training. It began by asking us to draw a picture of what makes a man a man and a woman a woman in this culture. The archbishop held up his picture of a warrior with a spear leading people into battle. 'A man is courageous,' he said. His picture of a woman was a face with a long tongue protruding from her mouth. He said, 'A woman gossips and interferes.' He went on to explain that a woman often stirs up trouble and this is why she must be disciplined by a man.

The training used just the Bible as its text. It started with Genesis and the creation account. Before the story of Eve coming from the rib of Adam, so often interpreted as saying that the woman is derived from and secondary to the man, there is the explicit creation of male and female made in the image of God, together and equally. By the end of the first day, one of the bishops broke down crying, his shoulders and body wracked with sobbing. We stopped, and through the tears he blurted out, 'I have just realised I am an abuser. If my wife has not got the dinner on the table when I get home or been working in the vegetable garden as I instructed, I discipline her. I understand now that this is what abuse actually is.' By the end of the course we asked them to draw what a man or a woman is in God's eyes and were amazed at completely different pictures of harmony and equality.

From its shameful treatment of sexual minorities to the exacerbation of some ethnic differences, at times the church has been anything but compassionate. I think of what the Jewish theologian and philosopher Martin Buber said, that 'nothing so tends to mask the face of God as religion'. I have seen Buddhist priests vilifying Rohingya and urging people to burn down their villages in Myanmar, and have stood in refugee camps on the outskirts of ISIS-occupied Mosul with Yazidis whose daughters were raped and carried off as slaves. I know that fear of others and the impulse to divide people into 'us' and 'them' is as 'natural' as compassion, existing in most if not all human hearts, and is perhaps a stronger temptation. When compassion in theory fails to translate in practice, I believe that what we are seeing is, at least in part, an identity problem.

Us vs them

To share a story, or a particular set of beliefs about the world and about what it is to be human, is to have a resource to draw on to strengthen and motivate compassion. But that shared story can equally become a means of marking off my people from others, and so blocking or limiting compassion.

Judaism has an identity founded upon the Exodus, the liberation of an enslaved people from Egypt through the compassion of Yahweh, who heard their cries and saw their oppression. Enshrined in the celebration each year of the Pesach or Passover is the reminder: we were once slaves, utterly vulnerable. The ethical content of the Jewish scriptures is undergirded by the experience. 'Remember that you were slaves in Egypt', reads the law (e.g. Deuteronomy 5:15, 24:17–22) as it commands the Israelites to treat the foreigner in their midst with dignity and justice.

The Exodus story is at once a universal story about a God of compassion and justice for the oppressed, and also a very particular, tribal story. Jean-Jacques Rousseau believed that Moses was the greatest leader in history because he took a bunch of runaway slaves and turned them into a nation, with an identity binding enough to sustain them as a people through conquest, exile, dispossession, and centuries of persecution. The genius to their identity is in telling and retelling their children who they are: slaves rescued by God and brought into the Promised Land. The story passes on the values by which they are to live – compassion, justice, and freedom – and provides the particular sense of identity that all humans need in order to undertake collective action.

Being part of a tribe in this way confers meaning and a secure basis from which to show compassion to the other. But its flip side can be an 'us vs them' mentality, which instead severs that connection to the other and becomes a barrier to compassion. The shadow side of the liberating Exodus story is the conquest and genocide carried out upon the inhabitants of Canaan. And the criticism of modern Zionism is that it celebrates further conquest. When Prime Minister Bibi Netanyahu declares that 'We will occupy all of Judea and Samaria', ancient place names for the small area left to Palestinians today, he invokes a conquest paradigm and a colonial settler mindset in the name of Israel's security. This attitude demonises Palestinians and denies them justice.

Fear of Palestinians can serve to entrench group identity in the Jewish diaspora, but it is at the cost of universal Jewish values. Zionism does not necessarily lead to harsh outcomes though. I am a patron of a Jewish-initiated project called Project Rozana. Started by Melbourne Jews, it funds and helps transport Palestinians from Gaza and the West Bank to receive medical treatment in Jerusalem's Israeli hospitals, which have world-class healthcare facilities. Palestinians, only a few kilometres away in the West Bank, have otherwise very rudimentary health care available to them, and little chance of access to anything better without an organisation like Project Rozana to negotiate the diplomatic red lines.

In the midst of COVID-19, this organisation has been frenetically sourcing ventilators within Australia for Palestinians and shipping them in. I see the particular Jewish identity of Melbourne Zionists manifesting in enormous compassion for 'the other', in keeping with the universal values they profess.

Who counts as the other? Who belongs within the circle of my compassion? A man I met once in

Beirut truly put flesh on the bones of this question for me.

In June 2013 I was visiting Syrian refugee camps in the Bekaa Valley in Lebanon. The scale of the war in Syria had seen six million refugees pour into Jordan, Turkey, and Lebanon. I was amazed that this small country had accepted more than a million refugees. They make up a quarter of its population.

After my visit, overwhelmed with the level of suffering I had seen, I went for a walk in Beirut to clear my head. It was about 10 pm and, wandering back to my bed, I heard a Lebanese voice greet me in broken English. A man was waving to me and inviting me into his home for a coffee. He introduced himself as Milak.

I entered Milak's front garden and saw a group of six refugees sitting around a fire and sharing coffee. 'Oh,' I said, 'You have guests, I should not stay.' He smiled and corrected me. They were not guests, but people living there and working in his solar panel business. He said they had been there six months and had nowhere else to go. I had just seen tens of thousands like them, living in tents with no work or future, sweating in summer and freezing in winter. He explained that we could talk freely as they did not speak English. Milak had learned the language from the nuns who had taken him in as an orphan and given him an education. He told me that was why he now identified as a Christian.

I knew a little about Middle Eastern politics and took a stab: 'I suppose you support President Assad?' Milak answered yes. He acknowledged that Assad was a butcher, but said that as a secular Alawite (belonging to the Shia minority), he would be more tolerant to Christians and other minorities than the Sunni rebels if they managed to oust him. 'If that happens,' Milak explained, 'then for religious minorities' – he ran a hand across his throat. So he was – with regret – supporting the lesser evil, he said, and shrugged.

I asked about the refugees he was now housing at personal cost and employing. 'Oh, they rise early, face Mecca, and pray to Allah for the Sunni rebels to win.' I was struck with such religious and political differences co-existing under one roof, and asked him why he had taken in people he passionately disagreed with. He paused and replied simply, 'Because they are vulnerable humans in need.'

As I sipped my coffee, the faces of the refugees watching us but unable to understand our conversation, a thunderbolt hit me. I was hearing afresh the ancient story of the Good Samaritan. In the next (and final) chapter, I want to unpack that story.

5. WHO IS COMPASSION FOR?

At the beginning of 2020 I chose to try being vegetarian.

I had been thinking about it for many years because I knew of the unnecessary suffering to both animals and people caused by meat-heavy diets. Commonly used methods of maximising production while minimising costs end up treating animals with great cruelty. The approximately 60 per cent of agricultural land worldwide that goes to grazing cattle and raising crops to feed them could, if directed towards plant-based farming and more plant-based diets, go to feed the world's 800 million hungry. And if we were not breeding 70 billion animals each year for the rich to eat, we could also set aside more land to renew the environment. As an exponent of compassion, I realised that my diet was not very compassionate towards animals, other humans, or the planet.

What surprised me most was the umbrage some of my friends took at the decision. They seemed to view it as a kind of personal betrayal.

Had I swapped them for a new 'tribe'? They assumed I must be judging them. (I wasn't, and I am absolutely comfortable dining with them as they tuck into a steak.) In Australia, where only five percent of us are vegetarian, it probably seems odder than in the UK and Germany (9%), Israel and Taiwan (12% and 13%), or India (nearly 40%). Nearly a billion people on the planet are vegetarian – though many by necessity, because of poverty. Those who choose vegetarianism out of compassion include adherents of Jainism, Hinduism, Rastafarianism, the Seventh-day Adventist Church, and Buddhism.

When I made the leap, I heard a lot of jokes about how the next stop is to become a fanatical vegan. Where do we draw the line? How do we decide who or what merits our compassion? These are questions that raise hackles. People get defensive.

Probably the most famous story Jesus told was in response to just this kind of question. A lawyer, who we are told was trying to 'test' Jesus, asked him to comment on the command 'Love your neighbour as yourself': 'And who is my neighbour?' Where are the limits? Who and what properly fall within the circle of my compassion? Who and what are excluded?

The Good Samaritan

This 2,000-year-old story is set on the road to the city of Jericho. A Jewish man is beaten up, robbed, and left for dead. An important detail in the story is that his assailants stole even his clothes, stripping him naked. Total humiliation, total abandonment. One of the implications of his nakedness is that the first passers-by – a priest and then a Levite – although also Jewish, would not have been able to tell if he belonged to their mob or not. Both refused to get involved and walked on by.

All of us know this compassion blocker at the back of our minds: this is not my problem, someone else will help, don't get involved. The natural compassion unblocker, bonds of shared identity, was unavailable without the cultural clue of the man's clothing. I wonder if these men would have stopped had they known he was one of their own.

The Samaritan who comes along next, of course, cannot tell the identity of the victim any more than the others could. But instead of asking *Is he one of us?*, he sees a vulnerable fellow human and stops to bind up his wounds. It does not stop there, either. Interrupting his journey and risking being mugged himself, the Samaritan puts the victim on his donkey to go and find an inn where he can be cared for and pays the full cost himself. He promises the innkeeper a blank cheque to feed and keep him until recovered – all for a stranger.

Love of the stranger is the first layer of Jesus' parable. Remember Peter Singer's question about our obligation to save the child drowning right in front of us *and* the child far away whose life we equally have the power to save. In the story, the injured man *is* right in front of the Samaritan (and the priest and the Levite). But he is also at a distance – he belongs to a different tribe. Surely he should be someone else's responsibility.

I know this logic only too well. I would be a rich man if I had a dollar for every Australian who has said to me, 'Tim, forget the needs of those overseas. Let's just look after our own.' In his 2014 budget, Prime Minister Tony Abbott smashed overseas aid and, when I protested, said to me, 'Look Tim, aid for the poor overseas is only for good times. We are not in good times and must look after Australians.' Other conservative leaders at the time, like David Cameron, did the opposite and increased aid, even though the United Kingdom had much higher public debt than Australia.

In reality, we have the capacity to do both – support the domestic poor and the poor overseas – and we should not set them up in a contest. The opposition is a false one not only because both are suffering and both deserve our compassion, but because the outcomes of aid are better for everyone. In December 2019, more than 150 federal politicians and ambassadors (including the US Ambassador) gathered for the launch of the Parliamentary Friends of the Pacific. I reminded Prime Minister Scott Morrison, the Leader of the Opposition Anthony Albanese, and both sides of parliament what General Jim Mattis as US Secretary of Defence had told President Trump when he tried to cut US aid: 'If you do this, you had better buy the military more bullets.'

The truth is that the poor, whether here or overseas, must fight for the crumbs from our table. Curiously, I have found that the people who argue most loudly to look to our own and cut foreign aid are commonly the ones doing least for the poor in Australia. When I was CEO of World Vision Australia and we did an audit of donors, I was surprised to find that the poorer postcodes gave more to World Vision than the richer postcodes. Maybe being closer to the threat of poverty triggers greater waves of compassion.

After I came back from responding to the Nepalese earthquake in 2015 that killed 9,000 people, I learned that homeless people in an outer eastern Melbourne suburb had taken up a collection to help the Nepalese. Our poorest here, helping foreigners in a nation they would never visit. They had seen stories of suffering on TV and gave out of the meagre amount of Newstart or a disability pension. I believe you learn compassion from responding to the needs of those who are our immediate neighbours, but I do not think compassion has a postcode beyond which it stops.

Beyond the pale

It is natural to love our own kind. It is not such a big leap to help someone we identify as 'like us' for any number of cultural reasons. To show compassion to the stranger, to someone who has no tribal claim on our loyalties, is a greater challenge. But there is an even more confronting layer to the story of the Good Samaritan: love of the enemy.

The mutual hatred between Jews and Samaritans was explosive. This foreigner who helped a stranger was not just an unlikely hero but actually an enemy of the man he saved. I think of Milak, showing hospitality to Sunni refugees who were political and religious enemies of the Christian minority.

Too often in my work I have had to go to places where ethnic hatred has exploded into violence. I remember attending the 10th anniversary of the Rwandan genocide. In 1994 nearly a million Tutsis were hacked to death in eight weeks by their Hutu neighbours. The two groups had been intermarried, all speaking the same language, intertwined communities. But the Belgians and the French, who as colonial masters had used divide-and-conquer tactics to accentuate tribal differences and privilege the Tutsis in education and opportunity, left a legacy of simmering discord. Radio propaganda by the dominant Hutus called the Tutsis insects and labelled them a threat to their neighbours and the nation. The killing that ensued was more systematic and efficient than the Nazis.

In the aftermath to mass murder, extra-judicial tribunals known as Gacaca courts or grass courts were established. This traditional form of communal justice was necessary simply to handle the caseload. Perpetrators who confessed their atrocities would receive a lighter sentence. Yet with the sheer number of offenders, this system too was grinding to a halt, and I discovered that something remarkable was happening: many survivors were choosing to forgive the alleged murderers even before they confessed. This surprising act of compassion for their enemies was a circuit-breaker. It opened a miraculous tidal wave of confession. After sentences were served, murderers were reintegrated back into the community. The national process of reconciliation that followed was scarcely believable. Ten years on, I sat with families who had established joint businesses between perpetrators and survivors.

What could reverse the human instinct for justice that forgiveness is only possible after confession? The survivors spoke of their Christian faith. They said that Christianity taught them to bless those who persecute you and to turn the other cheek. They believed that while they were still enemies of God, he had sent Jesus and purchased their forgiveness at the cross. If God forgives before we have confessed, they said, we must do the same.

The story of the Good Samaritan is an enactment of Jesus' teaching in what we call the Sermon on the Mount (found in chapters 5 to 7 of the Gospel of Matthew). The Beatitudes or blessings – *blessed are the poor, blessed are the meek, blessed are the peacemakers, blessed are you when people insult you and persecute you* – are a compassion manual. Jesus' most counter-cultural teaching in this whole scandalously counter-cultural sermon is to love your enemies.

Love of family and neighbour is hard enough. Enemies are to be, if not attacked, at least avoided. 'Tolerate your enemies' would be enough of a stretch, but *love* your enemies? This teaching only truly makes sense in connection with the cross, where suffering love is said to conquer power and hatred and revenge.

Someone who took love of enemies seriously was the Reverend Dr Martin Luther King Jr. As he and his fellow non-violent civil rights campaigners were jailed, beaten, their churches bombed, King wrote: 'We shall match your capacity to inflict suffering by our capacity to endure suffering ... Do to us what you will, and we shall continue to love you.' King consistently refused to attack and demonise his enemies. Even when humiliated, even after his own home was firebombed, he persisted in regarding those who persecuted him and his people as brothers and sisters.

While far from complete, King's dream can be said to have triumphed in many respects. Love can transform the enemy – but even if it does not, it shows compassion for the enemy. Of course, when you have love and compassion for your enemy, by definition they cease to be your enemy. As Abraham Lincoln reportedly replied to one who chastised him for not committing to the destruction of his political enemies, 'do I not destroy my enemies when I make them my friends?'

Who deserves our compassion? Who shall we include within the circle of our compassion? The neighbour? The stranger? The enemy?

These are radical and discomfiting questions, for the comfortable and for the wronged. But there is a further dimension to the question: Who is compassion *for*? We turn now, by way of conclusion, to the question of what it means to be the receiver as well as the giver of compassion.

CONCLUSION: BEING HUMAN

Years ago, I had an opportunity to observe at close quarters the life of Indian Hindus in the slums of Delhi. It was part of a video being made for TEAR Australia called *Unequal Worlds*, where I was comparing my life in Melbourne to life there. The stench, the oppressive heat, the noise of living in cardboard-thin hovels in dense confinement, not to mention no running water – it was literally a world away from mine. Girls would walk kilometres to a village well and carry jerry cans of water back, and even then it was water I could not drink.

But the play and chatter and vitality were what struck me. The narrowest street became a cricket pitch. The kids wanted me to play and laughed uproariously when I got bowled. Sheer radiant joy in play. And the religious temples served both as places of sanctuary, pockets of retreat where quiet could be found, and as places of colourful communal celebration, throbbing with energy on festival days.

Frankly, though, I could not survive long with

that noise and never again took for granted the simple blessing of running water. My youngest child, seeing the video, was blown away. If they don't have tap water because their homes don't have kitchens, he asked, then they must have a tap in a laundry or a backyard? I watched him grapple with unequal worlds, feeling deep compassion for those with less than him.

Some time later, I watched a UK documentary which brought Delhi slum-dwellers to London. It was their experiment in unequal worlds. For two weeks, they were shown around the great city: Westminster Abbey, the Tube, double-decker buses, Big Ben, Trafalgar Square, Buckingham Palace, recreation centres, famous cricket fields, and a few aged-care retirement homes. It must have been overwhelming and confronting for them – especially for those aware of how much of the city was built on imperial spoils from the period when England drained India of its wealth through the East India Company.

At the end of two weeks, before the visitors were to return home, the documentary-makers did extended interviews with each of them. What had their experience been like? Our Delhi slum-dwellers showed all the expected signs of culture shock, but they also said, 'We just feel so sad for the English. This is all so terribly sad.' The interviewer was taken aback. Sad? What could they mean? They explained what they had seen: so few kids playing on the streets. People unaware of each other, constantly in a hurry, rushing by without stopping and talking to each other. Worst of all was the way the English chose to put their old people all together in aged-care homes separate from their families, with their children only visiting them infrequently. How could they be so heartless? All of it was so alien to the warmth and laughter, the closeness of community back home. It was all so tragic, they said. What can we do to help these poor people in London?

As we think about compassion, it's easy to fall into the trap of seeing ourselves only as the people who *show* compassion to those other people, those who *need* it. Yet human frailty and vulnerability is universal. Everybody needs compassion, and everybody has the capacity to give it. It must be a two-way street.

The American writer and Trappist monk Thomas Merton said that 'Compassion is the keen awareness of the interdependence of all things'. If anything could teach us this, it was COVID-19. No respecter of borders or of social status, the virus turned all of us into potential carriers and reminded us that we are all biologically linked. From Tom Hanks to Boris Johnson, wealth and status are no protection. While anyone has it, all of us are potentially at risk. At 65, I know that my fate is in the hands of others, and particularly the younger generations.

Friends in Kenya told me of how the crisis began as a levelling force in their culture. Suddenly the rich were the ones being ostracised – the African poor saying we don't want to be around those who've been flying around the world and brought this virus here, you are a risk to us. Singapore did extremely well in the early stages of the pandemic and received global plaudits, but it failed to care for its migrant workers, housed in appallingly congested dormitories and forgotten, and a second outbreak tarnished its reputation as a global role model. A much more stringent lockdown followed for all citizens. Martin Luther King Jr famously said that 'Injustice anywhere is a threat to justice everywhere'. So coronavirus anywhere is a threat to all of us everywhere!

I believe that we were made for compassion. That to show compassion is to become more truly human, to discover a deep sense of purpose, to overcome our shallowness and competitiveness, our fear of abandonment and our fear of difference. In a world where polarisation is building and the climate changing, I believe our future depends on it.

NOTES

1. IS IT NATURAL?

Page 6: 'Lord, when did we see you hungry'. The parable of the sheep and the goats is found in Chapter 25 of the Gospel of Matthew. The upshot of this strange and confronting story of Jesus' is that when his followers serve the most overlooked and desperate people, they are in fact serving him.

Page 9: 'The fact, or at least the degree'. Quoted from the essay 'Son of Adam, Son of Man' in The Givenness of Things (Farrar, Straus and Giroux, New York, 2015).

Page 13: 'Christianity has taken the side'. This famous (or infamous) passage is from Nietzsche's *The Antichrist*, first published in 1895.

2. IS IT PRACTICAL?

Page 17: 'bowels of compassion'. Italics added.

4. IS IT POSSIBLE?

Page 38: 'an expressed principle'. Plotinus, *On Providence* 1.13.

Page 40: 'A human being is part of a whole'. You can read about this letter, from February 1950, at brainpickings.

org/2016/11/28/einstein-circles-of-compassion/.

Page 47: 'We will occupy all of Judea and Samaria'. See, for example, https://www.reuters.com/article/us-israel-palestinians/israels-netanyahu-says-he-wont-miss-west-bank-annexation-opportunity-idUSKBN2311I0.

5. WHO IS COMPASSION FOR?

Page 52: In Australia, where only five percent of us are vegetarian'. See https://www.worldatlas.com/articles/countries-with-the-highest-rates-of-vegetarianism.html.

Page 53: 'The Good Samaritan'. You can read the story in full in Chapter 10 of the Gospel of Luke.

Page 55: 'If you do this, you had better buy the military more bullets'. See https://www.washingtonpost.com/news/checkpoint/wp/2017/02/27/retired-generals-cite-past-comments-from-mattis-while-opposing-trumps-proposed-foreign-aid-cuts/.

Page 59: 'We shall match your capacity'. King expressed this sentiment on numerous occasions, and it can be found in the 1963 collection of his sermons titled *Strength to Love*.

Page 59: 'do I not destroy my enemies when I make them my friends?'. This quote is commonly attributed to Abraham Lincoln, but over the years a number of historical figures have been cited as the source, including Chinese and Roman emperors.

CONCLUSION: BEING HUMAN

Page 63: 'Compassion is the keen awareness'. Statement from Merton's final address, during a conference on East–West monastic dialogue, delivered just two hours before his death (10 December 1968).

Page 64: 'Injustice anywhere'. From King's *Letter from a Birmingham Jail* (April 1963).

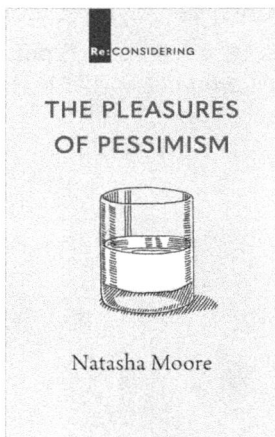

Pandemic, supervolcano, late capitalism, transhumanism, populism, cancel culture, the post-antibiotic age, the gig economy, the surveillance state, the cascading effects of climate change ...

Whatever the specifics, do you feel like things have gone off the rails – or are just about to?

If you've read the news, watched a zombie movie, or gotten into an argument on Twitter lately, the answer is probably yes.

And you're not alone.

What makes us such apocaholics?

What's so appealing about Armageddon? What are the pleasures – and also the perils – of our pessimism?